6
CARRIER AIR WING

Yves Debay & James Hill

CONCORD
PUBLICATIONS COMPANY
CONCORD COLOR SERIES

6
CARRIER-AIR WING

Front Cover

Armed and dangerous, this F-14 from VF-31, with an AIM-9 Sidewinder attached to its underwing pylons, is ready for action.

ISBN 962-361-706-2
Printed in Hong Kong

Back Cover

The USS FORRESTAL is a floating air base-a virtual seagoing airport. An unavoidable fact about aircraft is that in order for them to be able to fly, they must be maintained. The crewman whose silhouetted torso appears at the bottom of this photo can only briefly enjoy the magnificence of the Mediterranean sunset; his attention must shortly turn to the fork-tailed F/A-18 waiting for repairs.

The date of December 11, 1954 may not be the most memorable in the annals of the history of the United States Navy but it is nevertheless a significant one. That is the day that the world's first aircraft carrier built after World War Two - the USS FORRESTAL (CV-59)- was launched. When she was commissioned on October 1, 1955 at the Norfolk Naval Shipyard, FORRESTAL ushered in a new breed of aircraft carrier and a new era of naval warfare.

Christened in honor of James V. Forrestal, the United States' first Secretary of Defence, the FORRESTAL represented a series of "firsts" in carrier construction. She was the first "super carrier" designed and built specifically to operate jet-propelled aircraft. The FORRESTAL was the first American carrier to incorporate the British-developed angled flight deck, which allowed for simultaneous takeoffs and landings, and steam catapults (four instead of the usual two). She also featured four deck edge elevators to move aircraft from the hangar bays to the flight deck. While these attributes seem commonplace to us when we think about today's aircraft carriers, we should remember that they were revolutionary in the 1950s.

These distinctive features would soon appear on three other vessels in the new "FORRESTAL" class of aircraft carriers: the USS SARATOGA (CV-60), the USS RANGER (CV-61) and the USS INDEPENDENCE (CV-62).

The deployment history of the FORRESTAL was long and varied. In 1956, FORRESTAL was sent to the Mediterranean during the Suez Crisis to support the forces in that region. From 1958 to 1966, she alternated between the Second Fleet in the Atlantic and the Sixth Fleet in the Mediterranean.

In June of 1967, the FORRESTAL sailed from Norfolk for duty in the waters off the coast of Vietnam. After only five days of combat operations, a fire broke out on the flight deck which claimed 134 lives. This tragedy precluded any further activity in the area and forced the FORRESTAL to return to Norfolk for repairs.

The FORRESTAL deployed to the Mediterranean seven times between 1968 and 1975.

During America's Bicentennial celebrations in 1976, the FORRESTAL was Host Ship for the International Naval Review in New York City. President Ford rang in the nation's 200th birthday and reviewed over forty "tall ships" from the FORRESTAL's flight deck.

In March of 1981, the FORRESTAL was once again deployed to the Mediterranean, spending fifty-three days at sea during the Syria/Israel missile crisis. Tension was high in that region later that year during the Gulf of Sidra exercise and confrontations with Libyan aircraft resulted in two Libyan jets being shot down. The FORRESTAL's aircraft were credited with making more than sixty percent of all interceptions of Libyan aircraft.

From January 1983 to May 20, 1985, the FORRESTAL underwent a $550 million Service Life Extension Program (SLEP). SLEP is designed to modernize aircraft carriers and extend their lives at least another twenty years.

In June of 1986, the FORRESTAL sailed from her Florida port for her eighteenth Mediterranean deployment. In October of 1988, she completed her nineteenth major deployment after having operated in the North Arabian Sea, and in Mediterranean and North Atlantic oceans and logging 108 days at sea.

In July of 1991, the FORRESTAL made her last operational cruise and deployment to the waters off the coast of Turkey and Syria where she supported Operation "Provide Comfort" in Iraqi Kurdistan. The following October, the FORRESTAL participated in a NATO southern region exercise throughout the Eastern Mediterranean, the Aegean Sea and Turkey.

The FORRESTAL is slated to replace the USS LEXINGTON as the US Navy's training aircraft carrier in Pensacola, Florida in 1992.

As the saying goes, "old soldiers never die"; and this is certainly the case with the FORRESTAL. Her proud heritage will live on in the memories of military personnel and civilians, naval vessel and aircraft enthusiasts, and all those who remember her as a symbol of a strong and proud America.

Slicing through the waters of the eastern Mediterranean sea south of the Turkish coast, the USS FORRESTAL, its characteristic shape silhouetted against the horizon, presents a majestic appearance as the sun glistens in her wake. Because of the vastness of the surrounding Mediterranean, the enormity of the FORRESTAL is not immediately apparent . The view of the flight deck, which covers a total area of approximately four acres, gives a better indication of the carrier's overall size. Note the four catapult trails (upper right). The impressive length of the FORRESTAL is well illustrated in the lower left photo. The carrier is 1,039 feet long and would reach the 80th floor of the Empire State Building if stood on end. Note how the FORRESTAL seems to dwarf the French destroyer "Jean de Vienne", which provides an escort for the carrier while sailing in the eastern Mediterranean (lower right).

A view of the FORRESTAL's starboard bow as it sits in the harbor in Marseille, France during the Christmas of 1990. This vantage point shows just how massive the carrier really is. FORRESTAL weighs 80,000 tons and is as tall as a 25-story building when measured from keel to mast.

The clear blue sky over the harbor of Marseille and the colorfully painted tails of the two F-14 Tomcats of VF-31 sitting on the stern of the FORRESTAL's flight deck contrast sharply with the drab color scheme of the carrier, shown here undergoing repairs. The City of Marseille has a contract with the U.S. Sixth Fleet to help with the maintenance of its ships and FORRESTAL's crew is fortunate that allied countries like France provide harbor facilities so that much needed repair work can be performed. There are certainly less appealing locales in which to dock.

In this starboard view of the FORRESTAL (upper photo), an A-6 Intruder is being lifted up from (or lowered to) the hangar bay by one of the carrier's four elevators (lower left photo).It is the "island" superstructure, the command center of the FORRESTAL, seen rising from the starboard side of the flight deck, which draws most of our attention. Sheltered within this prominent tower, the commander of the FORRESTAL, sits in his seat on the navigation bridge (top row of windows in upper and lower right photo). Perched in the primary flight control station at the aft end of the island superstructure (seen in lower right photos right above the rotor blade hub of the SH-3H Sea King helicopter in the foreground), the Air Boss oversees all flight and deck operations. Note the numerous radar and communication antennae branching off from the mast and the island (lower photo). The FORRESTAL is equipped with 95 radio receivers and 75 radio transmitters.

The FORRESTAL is furnished with four 72 x 50 ft. elevators, three located on the starboard and one on the port side of the flying deck. Each is capable of lifting two aircraft. Photo shows an F/A-18 Hornet of the VFA-132 "Privateers" being transported by the front starboard elevator.

An F-14 Tomcat of VF-31 is lifted from the hangar bay to the flight deck. Notice how the wings are in high speed configuration while the plane is in transit. Note also the two external fuel tanks in the foreground . FORRESTAL's elevators are widely used for the transportation of ammunition, refuelling tanks and other equipment which can be removed from the flight deck and stored below.

The bridge of the USS FORRESTAL. It is here that the Captain, following the suggestion of the navigator, directs the ship's course. The Captain issues orders to the helmsman who, in the tradition of the earliest years of naval history, maneuvers the course by spinning a brass wheel.

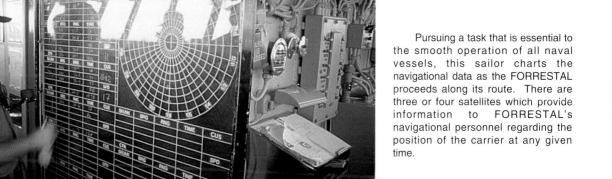

Pursuing a task that is essential to the smooth operation of all naval vessels, this sailor charts the navigational data as the FORRESTAL proceeds along its route. There are three or four satellites which provide information to FORRESTAL's navigational personnel regarding the position of the carrier at any given time.

The carrier air wing (CAW) attached to a task force is its main line of air defence. The aircraft in the CAW, with their anti-aircraft missiles, are usually more than capable of meeting any challenge. However, should enemy aircraft somehow get through this defence system, trained personnel aboard ship would then employ the quadruple Sea Sparrow sea-to-air missile system (shown here at the front starboard of the FORRESTAL).

The USS FORRESTAL boasts a crew of approximately 5000 personnel who are never idle and must be actively engaged in their duties twenty-four hours a day to insure the successful operation of the vessel. Each crew member works a shift of twelve hours on and twelve hours off—a grueling, but necessary, schedule. Normal flight deck activity aboard the FORRESTAL involves launches and recovery of aircraft at all hours of the day and night (the "peak" time being the afternoon), maintenance, refuelling and arming of the planes, and the storage of aircraft when the ship is in port.

Except for the Admiral (whose flagship is the carrier) and the commanding officer, who each have individual cabins, all of the officers live in cramped, Spartan spaces. The enlisted men sleep in bunks called "racks" stacked four or five deep between the deck and the seven-foot ceiling.

For the men who work below deck, the rotation of the earth is insignificant for they may not see the sun's light for a number of days. We have to admire their dedication to duty when we consider that they live in a world that is constantly subjected to the noise and din produced by the engine machinery and the launching catapults.

The flight deck is oblong in shape, smooth and featureless, with a tapering bow and stern. Work on the flight deck can be compared to an intricately choreographed, but highly hazardous ballet. Each member of the flight crew has a particular skill at which he excels and he must interact properly with the other members in order to insure the successful launch and recovery of each airplane. Failure to perform as required could result in a terrible and costly loss of aircraft and lives.

There are a number of responsibilities to perform on the flight deck and each crew member is as unique as his duties. For example, there is a great difference between the pilots who fly the aircraft popularized by the movie "Top Gun" and the young men (sometimes referred to as "deck monkeys") who work on the deck.

The individual roles aboard the FORRESTAL are clearly defined and on deck the color of each man's shirt and jacket indicates his function and his position in the hierarchy of duties. The most important people on the deck are the flight director and the catapult officers. They wear yellow jackets and are nicknamed "yellow dogs", probably because they bark their commands. The "yellow dog" has absolute authority on deck and nothing moves without his direction. It is the yellow jacket who gives the last signal before a pilot is launched from the catapult.

The deck hand in green hooks up the aircraft to the catapult and prepares it for launch.

The red-shirted ordnance men handle all kinds of weapons, missiles, and ammunition.

Purple clad deck crew members, called "grapes", are in charge of refuelling the aircraft.

The plane captain, identified by his brown jacket, is responsible for the cleanliness and operating condition of the aircraft under his charge.

Crewmen who inspect the aircraft as they approach the catapult wear white shirts. The black and white checkered pattern adorning their helmets and jackets, combined with their duty of checking the aircraft, explains why these men are sometimes referred to as "checkers".

A blue jacket on a crew member indicates that he operates the elevators, secures the aircraft to the deck with chains and chocks, and drives the tractors used to tow the planes.

From the time the US Marine Corps was established, Marines have been shipping out to sea to help preserve peace throughout the world. There are about sixty Marines stationed aboard the FORRESTAL to defend the ship and to perform security and police functions while at sea. One sobering responsibility they have, unknown to eighteenth century "leathernecks", is guarding the nuclear reactor (on nuclear-powered vessels) or any nuclear weapons that may be on board. Here a Marine keeps in shape by practicing a swift decent down a rope in the hangar deck.

One of the constant dangers of working on the flight deck is getting too close to the engine blasts of the aircraft. Here several crewmen huddle behind a tractor, or "mule", to stay out of harm's way as an A-6E Intruder passes by. The stenciled writing on the jacket worn by the yellow shirt in the foreground that he is responsible for directing the on-deck travels of the plane.

The variety of colors worn by this group of crew members assembled on deck between a launch and a recovery gives an idea of the many positions of responsibility held by the sailors on the FORRESTAL. Note the blue shirts with their yellow wheel chocks standing ready to secure an aircraft's tires. In the background, displayed on the island superstructure, is the large white vessel designation number "59" and the yellow winged anchors insignia that represents U.S. naval aviation. The ominous warning painted in yellow that also appears on the side of the island is clear evidence of the danger that each of these men faces in performing his task.

Here a multi-colored gathering of deck hands takes an opportunity to remove their helmets and sound suppressing equipment and enjoy a rare moment of quiet. Ever attentive to the business at hand, though, they listen intently as a "yellow dog" gives a security briefing.

The engine heat of this A-6E Intruder creates a mirage effect as the aircraft approaches for a landing. The crewmen on the left seem impressed with the sight even though it is not a new one to them. Having finished their respective jobs relative to this aircraft prior to its launch, all they can do now is watch its approach and hope for its safe recovery.

This photograph provides an excellent close-up view of the distinctive headgear worn by members of the flight crew. The helmet, called a "cranial" by the men, protects against head injury and provides relief from the oppressive noises that constantly assault the crew members' ears. Note the helmet's unique chinstrap. The need for eye protection is understandable when we consider the length of time these men spend on deck, coping with the glare of the sun rays directly and as they are reflected off the ocean's surface. The possibility of eye injury resulting from routine tasks is also very real.

Staying alert to the events around them, these green shirts wait for the catapult officers to guide this F-14 to its launch position. Once the aircraft is in place, they will secure its nosewheel launch bar to the catapult, readying the plane for takeoff.

Employing gestures reminiscent of a symphony orchestra conductor, this yellow-shirted catapult officer gives direction to the pilot as he awaits the signal to launch. The pilot's restricted field of view, and his inability to receive verbal commands due to the engine noise, require the flight directors to exaggerate their hand signals to avoid miscommunication. Once the order to launch is given (lower photo), the combined thrust of the steam catapult and the aircraft's engine hurl the plane off the deck. The whole procedure is then repeated with another aircraft. Note the six sections of the jet blast deflector shield in position behind the F/A-18 Hornet.

A catapult officer and two green shirts prepare to send this S-3 Viking on its way (upper photo). A red-shirted fire fighter also watches the launch intently and hopes that his services will not be needed. It is the responsibility of these green shirts to determine exactly how much steam pressure is required to safely and successfully launch each aircraft. Their calculations are relayed to the steam operators below deck, who adjust the pressure accordingly.

The pilot of this F-14 seems to be saying, " Take good care of my Tomcat." Responsible for its cleanliness and good working order, these two brown-shirted plane captains no doubt feel the same attachment and bond of devotion to the aircraft placed in their care as members of the ground crews from WWI to the Gulf War have felt about the aircraft they serviced.

It is up to the white shirts in these photos to inspect the aircraft as they are made ready for hook-up on the catapult. They brief a pilot of an S-3 Viking (lower photo) and bring an EA-6B Prowler to launch position (upper photo). The checkered pattern on these security officer's jackets is clearly visible in both of these photos.

These red shirts use one of many yellow dollies to transport a Sparrow missile to an awaiting Tomcat. It is obvious that these two ordnance men take their jobs seriously and are aware of the danger involved in handling and moving munitions; even in a still photograph their concentration is apparent.

Shadows grow long as this brown shirt, laden with chains, awaits his call to secure an aircraft to the deck. The casual air of the blue shirt and red shirts in the background seems to indicate that the frantic pace that is so characteristic of launches and recoveries seems to have subsided.

A blue shirt, having hooked up the front wheel of this F/A-18 Hornet to the tow bar, steers his mule to lead the aircraft to the elevator as the brown-shirted plane captain sitting in the pilot's seat controls what movement he can. These yellow tractors must be able to maneuver around (and under the wings of) a multitude of styles of planes. It is easy to see from this photo how the mule's low profile would make this easier to do.

Looking more like a member of the maintenance crew than a security officer, this "checker" lends a helping shoulder and hauls a tank of liquid oxygen to a nearby Tomcat. Notice the three brown-shirted plane captains at left busying themselves with the routine upkeep of "their" plane. The willingness of each crewman to put 110% of himself into his daily performance is one reason that the flight deck operations aboard the FORRESTAL run so smoothly.

Sailors aboard the FORRESTAL consider the a meal to be the "number one" priority following the completion of their shifts. An army of cooks is constantly on duty in the carrier's galley and it is possible to eat at anytime, twenty-four hours a day. The galley serves 22,000 meals each day and the daily fresh water use is about 30,000 gallons. Unlike the Royal Navy and the French Navy, however, no alcohol is served on board the FORRESTAL.

The brief period of rest first thing in the morning is an excellent time to take in some exercise. Jogging around the flight deck is an activity favored by some of the crew members; another popular "track" is below in the hangar deck. Flight deck operations is mentally demanding and physically taxing. It is best suited for the younger sailors and those crewmen who are able to maintain the stamina necessary to overcome fatigue.

Mental exertion can take a toll on the body and it is sometimes necessary to relax and unwind. Here a sailor, sitting under the tail of a Prowler extending over the edge of the deck, takes a well-deserved break and reflects on the day's events and life at sea. Surrounded by an ocean extending as far as the eye can see in every direction, a crew member can easily feel alone, even though there are thousands of other personnel aboard.

This Mediterranean sunset might stir memories of spouses and sweethearts, but the crewmen must suppress those thoughts as best as possible and carry on with the task at hand.

"Safety First"

Since the great fire that damaged the FORRESTAL 1967 in Vietnam, the authorities in charge of the carrier have been justifiably preoccupied with the safety on board the vessel. Consequently, a great many safety measures are taken and different safety exercises are conducted on the ship.

Dressed in shiny fire-resistant suits, these fire fighters keep an alert vigil over the activities on deck. Aware of the history of the FORRESTAL, they will do everything in their power to prevent another disaster like the fire that took the lives of so many crewmen in 1967. The way in which the fire fighter in right photo holds his helmet in his arms illustrates the bulkiness of the fireproof gear. Knowing how hot these suits must be even when the red shirts are just resting, one can only imagine how unbearable it must be to wear one while fighting a fire.

The FOD (Foreign Object Damage) walkdown is one precautionary measure that takes place before a series of launches can begin. As shown here, everyone— deck hands, Marines, pilots, and any other available body— forms a line across the width of the deck and walks shoulder to shoulder from bow to stern, scanning the deck surface for any loose object, such as a piece of metal, screws, wire, etc., which could be sucked into the engines of an aircraft and cause damage to them.

This green-shirted deck hand performs his job in dangerously close proximity to the propellers of a C-2 Greyhound. This is merely one example of the hazardous working conditions faced by the crew members. Heeding the continuous reminders to be cautious and following safety instructions are two ways these sailors reduce the risk of injury.

Several crewmen, sporting work jerseys of all colors, participate in an anti-fire exercise. Their assistance in a real emergency will enable the red-shirted fire fighters to more effectively perform the risky business of approaching a flame-engulfed aircraft to rescue the pilot. Notice how the yellow tractor can be used as a lift to raise the fire fighters up to an aircraft's canopy just for this purpose. While these men are shown practicing with fire hoses, water would only be used in the case of a non-fuel fire.

Seen here during a crash drill, fuel-pumping "grapes", green-shirted maintenance workers and two brown shirts are poised alongside their stretchers, ready to evacuate a wounded pilot. In upper photo, all types of crewmen scramble toward the special crash barrier net, made of strips of nylon webbing, which has been erected to help restrain an aircraft as it makes an emergency landing. The red and white fire truck (center) and the multi-purpose tractor are both essential on-deck equipment in the event of an emergency.

Following the drill, everyone pulls together (literally) and helps to fold up the barrier net. As with all their endeavors on the flight deck, these crewmen put forth a maximum effort to get the job done. It is no small feat to secure the net and each man's muscles strain as he does his share of the labor. Having finally wrestled it into a position where it can be transported more easily, this colorful parade of crew members hauls away the folded net so it can be stored in its place below deck.

These men inside the flight control station, located at floor level in the FORRESTAL's superstructure, are in charge of plotting the movement of the aircraft on the flight deck and planning their movement to a launch position or to the storage bay, depending on the schedule. The complex series of moves on deck is rehearsed in miniature on this table, which almost gives the impression that a sophisticated board game is in progress. Orders for movement of the aircraft are transmitted to the flight deck officers who receive the communication through their cranials by means of a two-way FM radio head phone set called a "mouse" (so named due to its resemblance to Mickey Mouse).

Each squadron of aircraft on board the FORRESTAL has its own "ready room" where the pilots prepare themselves for the mission. In this room, the commander briefs the crews as to which radio frequency they will tune to, the type of ammunition they will be using, the load of fuel to be pumped into their planes, the grid for refuelling place, etc. Following this briefing, the pilots take some time to study their maps and review their mission.

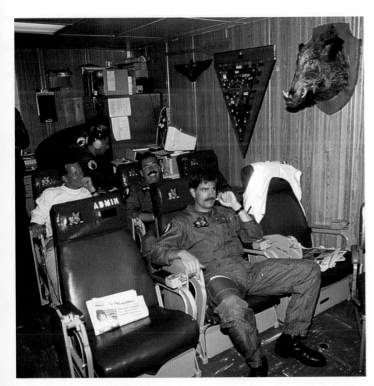

While the pilots are being briefed, the aircraft chosen for the next launch are towed to a specially designated spot near the island, or to an area on the rear fueling deck near the ship's stern, where they are armed and prepared for flight. Just as soon as the blue shirts have unchained this F/A-18, they will hook it up to a mule and tow the aircraft to the mission preparation area. On route, the brown-shirted plane captain in the cockpit will ride the break and steer "his" plane. This angle provides an overhead view of a Hornet that is not often seen.

Two F/A-18s that are armed and ready for action. These two brown shirts are fastidious in their efforts to insure the cleanliness of the aircraft they service, bestowing one last bit of attention to the Hornet prior to pilot climbing aboard (upper photo). These planes have already been armed with Sidewinder and Sparrow missiles. While the flight director communicates with the flight deck control center below deck, the blue-shirted mule drivers wait for the yellow shirt to direct them to their next destination on the flight deck.

With their folded wings and V-shaped tails, these F/A-18s present quite an angular picture as they wait to be towed to to the rear of the flight deck. While one has received a pair of Sidewinders, the other must wait for the red-shirted munitions experts to affix its weapon load. The nature of each mission determines what kind of ordnance each plane will carry.

While a mule and a red-tailed Tomcat of VF-31 pass in review on the rear starboard deck area behind them, the planes in the foreground provide silent testimonial to the success of the space-saving qualities of the folding wings of carrier aircraft. The traffic situation on the FORRESTAL's flight deck during pre-launch maneuvering makes it essential to keep as many aircraft out of the way and as close together as possible. Through the combined efforts of the flight directors and the other crew members, the aircraft scheduled for each mission end up where they should be, when they should be, and the carrier's launch activity proceeds according to plan.

When the armament load for a mission has been decided, it is up to the ordnance men to assemble the variety of missiles and ammunition and arm the planes with them. In these views, red shirts convoy and load several types of weaponry. In upper photo, two red shirts steer a cart loaded with Sidewinder missiles is guided toward a row of awaiting aircraft. Upper right photo shows just what kind of effort it takes to load a Sidewinder missile onto the wing tip of an F/A-18 of the VFA-137 "Kestrels". Two ordnance men roll a cart full of Sparrow missiles past an Intruder of VA-176 "Thunderbolt" in lower right photo. Here (lower photo) an Intruder receives a special kind of armament—an air-to-ground "smart' bomb.

The aircraft on the FORRESTAL are also armed with more conventional weaponry. For example, some planes are equipped with the internally mounted Vulcan M61A1 20mm rotary cannon. The strange yellow (what else?) contraption shown here is the device used to load up the 20mm shells into the gun's magazine, which can hold 1000 rounds on some aircraft. Note the black belt of ammunition winding its way up to the gun mount in the port side fuselage of this F/A-18.

Final preparations are being performed on this A-6 of the "Thunderbolts" prior to its launch. With a conscientious effort to provide the pilot with good visibility from the outset of the mission, this brown shirt puts the finishing touches on cleaning the Intruder's canopy and windscreen. Note the red fold-down ladders that assisted the plane captain up to the cockpit.

With everything ready to go, the pilots head toward their planes. The Prowler crew seen here (upper left photo) begins the delicate procedure of fitting the pilot into the cockpit. Before these pilots board their aircraft, they take a pre-launch walk around the planes. Assisted by other crew members, they check the missile load and all movable surfaces of the planes, and examine any internal work that has been performed on the aircraft. The pilot of an Intruder checks the refueling tanks (upper right photo). The pilot of the F-14 (lower left photo) inspects the Sidewinder missile on his wing glove pylon. Notice the yellow protective cap on the missile's nose. After finishing the pre-flight check of his Tomcat, this fighter pilot climbs into the cockpit (lower right photo). The hoses, pouches, belts, etc. protruding from his special flight suit are designed for the pilots' survival against the G-force strain he will encounter during the launch and while flying.

A study of pilots as they wait out the moments prior to launching. The two pilots of these F/A-18s (upper and lower photos) present a frightful and fearless demeanor behind their oxygen masks and tinted helmet visors. The only way to distinguish them from one another once they are suited up for flight is by the name painted beneath the canopy. Hornet "401" has achieved a bit more individuality by displaying the small red and blue cowboy seen painted on the nose. The plane captain in charge of this Intruder (left photo) makes some last minute adjustment for the bombardier/navigator prior to the order to proceed to a catapult.

Just above the tops of their helmets (upper left photo), attached to their headrests, are the handles of the Martin-Baker ejection seats. The orange and red markings on the helmets worn by these crewmen, and those in the Tomcat (lower photo), lend a noticeable splash of color to the otherwise mottled and drab surroundings. Strapped into their seats, their helmet visors lowered to their oxygen masks, these pilots look to the catapult crew for the OK to launch.

Under the direction of the catapult officer in yellow, colorful Tomcat "201" of VF-31 slowly proceeds to the catapult ; the green shirts and fire fighters walking alongside also help to supervise the pre-launch movement of the aircraft. Considering the potential for mishap and injury should any aspect of the launch go wrong, it is easy to understand why each of these crew members shows the concern he does.

Diverse aircraft of the FORRESTAL's CAW-6 are shown here as they approach their respective catapults. The flight captains in yellow stand well away from the aircraft they direct in order to insure that the pilots can see their gestures. The F-14 of the "Red Rippers" squadron (upper right photo) taxies to position past ever-present yellow tractors as an F/A-18 Hornet begins its ascent from the waist catapult. Hornet "400" (lower photo) belongs to the squadron leader of VFA-137.

This E2-C Hawkeye is ready to be attached to the bow catapult. Through his hand signals, the flight officer has notified the pilot that the time has come to move forward. With its propellers just beginning to spin and it wings still retracted, the Hawkeye starts to taxi. The Sea King helicopter flies above the carrier during each launch. In the event that a mishap occurs, it is ready to perform a rescue mission.

An A-6 Intruder of VA-176 is all hooked up at the waist catapult and ready to go once the cat officer gives the signal to launch. One eye-catching feature of Navy aircraft is the red paint applied behind the leading edge slat and inside the flaps to alert cremen of moving parts. At what seems to be a dangerously close distance to the exhaust of the A-6, a"Tomcatter" of VF-31 waits his turn for takeoff near the edge of the deck.

This Intruder rolling to the catapult has just unfolded its wings. These bombers carry more external fuel tanks than other aircraft and are normally launched early because they have a longer fuel autonomy. While some A-6s in the squadron have switched to the subdued tail markings, Intruder "523" boldly displays the high-visibility version of the squadron insignia of VA-176 (the red lightning bolt clutched in a mailed fist).

With the pilot of the aircraft obscured from view, this Tomcat (upper photo) appears to have taken on a life of its own. The yellow shirt seems more like a trainer as he directs the 'cat' on its way. An F/A-18 (left photo) maneuvers itself toward the starboard catapult as two green shirts eyeball the catapult to insure its proper working order in final preparation for the Hornet's hook-up. As the white shirts begin their security check, the ordnance men in red approach the aircraft. They wait until the very last moment before activating the armament attached to the plane.

The key to a successful launch is to adhere to the final instructions given by the yellow-shirted flight director. Accordingly, the pilot of this Hawkeye (left photo) follows the lead of the catapult officer as the plane taxies toward the launching site. The wings of the E2-C aircraft will remain folded until the final moments prior to launch. There is no question as to where the catapult officer want this Intruder to go (lower photo). With its nosewheel tow bar raised preparatory to hook-up, the aircraft rolls to the catapult for its ascent toward the sun, the blinding glare of which is reflecting off the light-colored clothes worn by the catapult officer.

With the massive island superstructure serving as an impressive backdrop, this F/A-18 (upper photo) acts out the final dramatic moments of its pre-launch drama the unfolding of its wings. The numerous crewmen in the background serve only as an ensemble cast as the Hornet takes center stage at the hook-up position at the bow catapult (right photo). Note that there is already vapor escaping through the deck's launch path as steam pressure builds for the launch.

Considering that a launch just took place at the neighboring catapult (as indicated by the steam in upper photo), it is unlikely that the green shirt waiting on this Tomcat will hear the remarks that this catapult officer seems to be shouting to him. At center, the two white shirts standing atop the unraised blast deflector shields appear to be making a close examination of the pitot tube on the nose of the F-14. Having crossed over the unraised blast deflectors, this "Red Rippers" Tomcat (left photo) is now under the control of the catapult hook-up crewman and the catapult officer. In not many seconds it will be airborne.

Almost lost among the various radar and flag lines that cut geometric paths through the sky, the national colors fly overhead. The black ball and diamond-shaped signal (at bottom) are raised into the mast's rigging as a notification that that everything is "Go" for the launch of an aircraft.

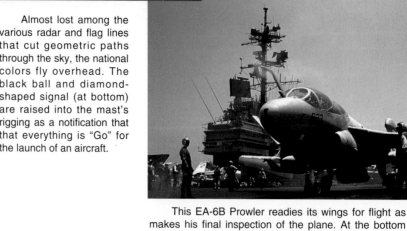

This EA-6B Prowler readies its wings for flight as the security officer makes his final inspection of the plane. At the bottom right of the scene, next to the red shirt, is the catapult launch panel manned by its green-shirted operators, called "shooters". As soon as the shooter has confirmed that everything is clear for takeoff, he'll press the launch button which signals the catapult operators to fire, and then it's up and away for this Prowler.

Having completed their pre-flight checklist, the pilot and RIO (Radar Intercept Officer) sit in the cockpit of their F-14 and wait for their turn to be hooked-up. Adding to the F-14's unique profile is the Northrop television camera sight (TCS) located directly under the nose.

Shrouded in the fog of a previous launch, catapult crewmen prepare F/A-18 Hornet "400" of the VFA-137 "Kestrels" (upper photo) for hook-up at the bow catapult. A green shirt scrambles in to handle the hook-up details while observant white shirts and red shirts scrutinize the aircraft. Hornet "401" (lower two photos) follows closely behind with flaps lowered to increase air resistance. Once its engines are cranked up and the OK is given, this bird will soar over the edge of the deck and up to the clouds.

With the heat-scorched deflector shield raised to protect men and machine from the violent blast and searing wind of each launch, the hook-up procedure gets underway (upper photo). The green-shirted hook-up man has affixed the nosewheel launch bar to the catapult shuttle (lower photo) and has secured the break-away holdback bar (seen aft of the nosewheel) to the deck, and now he signals for increased tension in the launch bar. Once the green shirt scurries clear of the aircraft, the F/A-18 will be ready to be thrust skyward.

This E2-C receives guidance from the flight officer as he approaches the launch position (upper photo). Final hook-up activity nears completion (lower photo) and the yellow-shirted flight officer makes one of his less elaborate gestures to the pilot. Note the impressive wing span of the E2-C; it exceeds eighty feet. Despite the aircraft's large size, the catapult will have no difficulty in sending Hawkeye "603" on its way.

The bulbous nose of Intruder"523" dominates this view of the hook-up procedure and dwarfs the crewmen plying their special skills at the nose-wheel below. Inside his cockpit, the pilot of the A-6 (upper right photo) keeps his attention riveted on the gestures of the flight captain (or, perhaps, the photographer). The catapult shuttle can be seen racing through the cloud of steam as it returns to the hook-up point following the previous launch (upper left photo).

This long shot of a C-2 Greyhound transport plane being positioned for launch serves well to illustrate just how many personnel can become involved in the launching of an aircraft. Apart from the several crew members at right who remain close to the the aircraft before it is catapulted, notice the numerous crewmen at left assembled at the edge of the flight path.

The hook-up of this S-3 Viking anti-submarine aircraft appears to be going along without a hitch. As the time for launch nears, the plane's wings will unfold to a length of nearly 70 feet. This pre-launch pose affords the flight officer a good view of the aircraft's twin TF34 turbofan engines and two external fuel tanks. These will serve to assist the Viking as it soars from the flight deck and extend its flight while airborne.

A flight director holds his fists together in the "brakes on" gesture to the pilot of this F/A-18 (upper photo) as instruction to stabilize the plane for hook-up prior to the building up of steam in the catapult. As soon as the flight director has ceased his series of gestures and the hook-up man has completed his task, this F/A-18 will get the "go ahead" signal for launch.

Under the tutelage of a patient and capable veteran deck hand, this young green shirt learns the proper method of holding up the weight board, the device which displays the estimated weight of the aircraft being launched. After the pilot has confirmed the accuracy of the number, it is shown to the catapult operators so they will know how much steam pressure is needed for the launch. It must be unnerving for new deck hands to try to absorb all of the information coveyed to them in such a hectic and noisy "classroom" as an aircraft carrier's flight deck.

The catapult operator (in green, wearing the striped helmet) gives the "thumbs-up" sign and the catapult officer drops to one knee, signaling to the Hornet that it is time to commence the launch(upper left photo). A duo of catapult officers, their arms outstretched toward the edge of the flight deck, give their final signals to the pilot (upper right photo). Visible at the center of the deck, a group of miscellaneous crew members has gathered near a fire truck to offer moral support to the pilot and to watch the aircraft roar past.

Sign language as practiced aboard the FORRESTAL. This green shirt sprinting clear of the catapult path holds up his gloved hand to alert the cat officer that he has successfully hooked-up this "Gamblers" Viking to the bow catapult (left photo). With a motion that is considerably low-key for a flight director, the "Maestro" salutes the pilot before he launches. This S-3 will soon be hurled down the catapult while the raised deflector shield protects crewmen and other aircraft from its engine blast. You can almost read the minds of these two catapult officers as they direct this E2-C Hawkeye (lower photo) on its way......Go! Go! Go!   At right, a security officer and a fire fighter observe the launch proceedings.

Once the pilot of Tomcat "212" of VF-31 has received the OK from the flight officer and the catapult officers (upper and middle photos), he must prepare himself for the G-force pressure that will assail him during the launch. The aircraft, too, undergoes a gruelling physical challenge at this time. The engines are cranked up to the maximum after the nosewheel is compressed and secured to the catapult by the nosewheel launch bar and launch holdback bar. While the engines are revved up, the brakes remain engaged. The aircraft (especially the nosewheel strut) is thus subjected to intense physical stress, relieved only when the strain causes the holdback bar to break and the aircraft actually launches.

The "Maestro" is in rare form as he conducts the launching of the most colorful F-14 on board the FORRESTAL, Tomcat "201" of VF-31. In just a matter of seconds this Tomcat has raced down the 300 foot length of the catapult rail, reaching a speed of 160 mph. With its afterburners aglow and its wings outstretched, this Tomcat will soon rise into the clear sky over the Mediterranean.

As it clears the edge of the flight deck and soars heavenward, Tomcat "505" is in full afterburner. Each of the F-14's Pratt & Whitney TF30 turbofan engines can produce 20,900 lbs. of thrust. Here, the intense heat they generate affects the surrounding air, lending a dreamlike quality to the event. The mood ends quickly, though, as the rumbling that emanates from the powerful jet engines rouses all but the most weary from any dream-producing slumber.

Sailing over the edge of the waist catapult, this Tomcat finishes the last phase of the launch and climbs into the sky over the waters off the coast of Turkey to begin its patrol of Kurdistan. The aircraft will soon take on a much more sleek appearance, or "clean up", when it retracts its landing gear.

Shrouded in the foggy mist of the residual steam from an earlier launch, this F-14 wastes no time in moving up to the catapult to take his turn (left photo). The fact that the carrier's catapult crews are capable of launching a dozen aircraft within a 10-minute period attests to their skill. A carrier like the FORRESTAL may have aircraft launching, in the sky, or on approach for recovery at any time of the day or night. Tomcat "212" of VF-31's "Tomcatters" (right photo) is poised for launch nose compressed, flaps down, engines fired up and cottony billows drifting from the catapult rail evince the build-up of the steam pressure necessary for the launch.

A view from the navigation bridge in the island superstructure shows a different perspective of the launch sequence. From this vantage point, an observer can see all four of the catapults in action at the same time. As crowds of crew members gather to oversee and watch the launch of this F-14 (middle photo), the orange afterburners blaze against the erected deflector shields (seen here from behind, raised by the hydraulic lift arms). As puffs of steam drift upward from the catapult rail (lower photo), the Tomcat clears the deck and veers away from the bow. Another aircraft launched just moments earlier can be seen at a higher altitude in the sky above the middle of the horizon line.

With the assistance of the waist and bow catapults, these F/A-18s roar toward the edge of the flight deck, their engines thrusting them upward. Near the end of the waist catapult, a red shirt leans nonchalantly on the rail alongside a row of life rafts (lower photo), seemingly oblivious to the noisy, yet graceful takeoff performed by the pilot of this Hornet. Due to the width of the FORRESTAL's flight deck, the Hornet rising from the waist catapult (next page, upper photo) seems to be a scale model in comparison to this S-3 Viking all hooked up and ready to soar off of the bow catapult.

Indicating yet another successful launch, catapult steam hugs the deck, partially obscuring the several crew men who are interested in the upcoming flight of a member of the "Privateers" squadron. The object towering in the background is the Belknap pole; it has a navigation light on top which indicates to surrounding vessels the direction the FORRESTAL is travelling.

The waters of the Mediterranean sea frame this classic illustration of aircraft carrier launch procedures (upper photo). In the right foreground, an F-14 and an Intruder await transportation to the site where they will be prepared for flight. While the S-3 Viking lifts off from the waist catapult, an F/A-18, with hook-up complete, awaits his chance. Another Hornet wheels up behind the deflector shields and will taxi to the hook-up position once the other aircraft has finally cleared the bow (middle left photo). The insignia red paint within the flap surfaces catches the viewer's eye as this A-6 Intruder awaits and executes its launch (lower right and lower left photos).

The launch from the waist catapult of Intruder "507" of the VA-176 "Thunderbolts", viewed from "Vulture's Row" (an observation area on the port side of the island). Notice the folded, overlapping wings of the sub-chasing S-3 Vikings waiting to be towed (foreground of middle photo).

From the navigation bridge, we enjoy an unobstructed, bird's-eye view of the launch of an E-2C (upper photo). It presents an imposing sight as it receives its last signal from the flight director. The substantial size (24 ft. in diameter) of the Hawkeye's rotodome, referred to as the "frisbee", is clearly visible from this angle. The twin Allison turboprop engines leave behind their noted streams of smoke, mingling with catapult steam as the plane nears the edge of the flight deck (lower left photo); the smoke is only faintly visible in this eerie and spectral view of shadow puppet deck crewmen watching the Hawkeye's ascent (lower right photo).

An inbound EA-6B Prowler makes its final approach for landing, lining up for a "trap" on the deck of the FORRESTAL. Landing a 30-ton aircraft on the deck of a moving aircraft carrier is the greatest challenge in naval flying operations. To the credit of all personnel involved, it is an achievement that occurs hundreds of times, both day and night, during a carrier's deployment. As the pilot directs the aircraft into the glidepath (the line of descent to a landing), he is aided in his landing by the Fresnel Lens Optical Landing System, more commonly known as the "ball". It is a series of horizontal green lights, representing the level deck, and vertical red lights, indicating the plane's position in relation to the deck, located at the port side of the stern. One glance at the ball and the pilot knows if he is lined-up correctly for recovery (green lights), or if he is too high or too low (red lights).

All set to make a landing, the EA-6B has its landing gear down, its wing flaps lowered, and the split wing-tip speed brakes fully open. The pilot has also lowered the arresting hook, or tail-hook, from the tail of the plane. As the aircraft lands, it will drag behind and latch on to one of the four arresting cables which span the width of the rear deck.

This is the view that a deck crewman would have of an S-3 Viking as it lines up prior to its recovery (upper photo). The yellow-jacketed flight director strikes an exultant pose to express to the pilot of the Viking that he has executed a flawless landing (right photo).

Having come in a little high on the approach, this F-14 of the "Red Rippers", its tailhook still dangling, zooms over the heads of several unconcerned crew members and soars back up into the air to make a second attempt at a landing. Such an action is referred to as a "bolter". Sometimes a plane comes in for recovery a little long, or the tailhook hops over the arresting cables. In anticipation of such a mishap, aircraft carrier pilots push the throttle forward as they near the deck and "rev" the engines up to "take off" power so they can go around for another try, if necessary. If a proper trap is effected, the throttle is merely returned to the "idle" position.

In the groove—a perfect recovery. This "Tomcatter" of VF-31 shows us just how it's supposed to be done. Three of the four arresting cables are visible in this shot as gray-brown lines that transverse the deck in front of the approaching F-14 (upper left photo). As the Tomcat's wheels touch down, they create a small puff of smoke (upper right photo), and the aircraft completes its recovery. The tailhook is now drawn back into the carriage of the aircraft, the arresting cable, having been yanked and twisted by the hook, returns hydraulically to its original position at the stern, and a flight director herds the aircraft to a parking place at the bow of the vessel (lower photo).

The key player in all phases of the recovery is the LSO, the Landing Signal Officer. He is a veteran pilot who, positioned at an observation platform at the stern of the carrier, has a clear view of the aircraft as it lines up for recovery and communicates by phone with the approaching plane to offer guidance and criticism to its pilot. Each squadron has its own LSO and there are commonly six or more people on the LSO platform: the duty LSO, a couple of LSOs-in-training, and radiomen who receive and transmit messages throughout the ship for the LSO. The telephone used by the LSO connects him to the Air Boss, the CCA (Carrier Controlled Approach), which is the air traffic control center on the ship, and the pilot of the inbound planes.

LSOs pay close attention to every aspect of this F/A-18's landing. If it seems to the LSO that the plane is lined up properly for recovery, his remarks to the pilot are minimal; if something appears amiss about the approach, the LSO will, as diplomatically as possible, offer correction and constructive criticism. When there is a reason to abort the landing altogether, the LSO will "wave off" the pilot and send him back up again for a new approach by pushing the button of the pickle switch carried in his right hand which causes the red lights of the ball to illuminate.

This F-14 of the "Red Rippers" appears suspended in air behind the busy green shirt as it bolts back up into the sky above the FORRESTAL(upper photo). On its second pass, it achieves a successful trap (lower photo). The black line cutting through the ocean at the left is the arresting cable, still snagged by the Tomcat's tailhook.

Once back on the deck, following the recovery, this Tomcat is no longer the concern of the CATCC (Carrier Air Traffic Control Center) who had monitored his movement in the skies above the FORRESTAL. After returning to the ship, the F-14 is once again in the jurisdiction of the flight director. The pilot now looks to the yellow shirt for instruction on where to go next.

One of several F/A-18s of the "Kestrels" which performed a perfect trap of the third arresting cable after completing a patrol over Kurdistan. This is considered a commendable performance even during a series of "touch and go" practice landings much less following a fatiguing "real life" flight operation. It is almost a sure bet that these recoveries might not have gone so smoothly if it had been nighttime or if the weather were inclement, when visibility is decreased and the pilot's stress level is greater .

On their final approach, some F/A-18s "dirty up", abandoning the sleek, "clean" appearance they display in flight by lowering the tailhook, landing gear and flaps. We can almost hear the LSO's command to the pilots of these Hornets to "Call the ball" and adjust their positions as they line up in the glidepath behind the FORRESTAL. It is a reminder that these planes are landing on the deck of a moving vessel, not a runway on land, and that increased levels of skill and concentration are therefore required. A tail view of Hornet "401" of the "Kestrels" moments after its recovery (lower photo). The thick wire arresting cable which brought this F/A-18 to a violent, lurching halt appears to be as weak as filament, having been lifted almost level with the bottom of the exhaust nozzles when hooked; here the cable has not yet fallen from the plane's tailhook.

These F/A-18s of the "Privateers" and the "Kestrels" squadrons illustrate the sequence of events that immediately follows a recovery. After the arresting cable, which is still trapped here (lower left photo), is dropped, the aircraft taxies away from the landing area under the direction of a flight director. So that the recovered aircraft will not be an obstruction to incoming planes, the pilot will fold up its wings and park his plane in some secluded area out of the way of the soon-to-be-landing fellow aviators. Notice the stack of wheel chocks piled off to the side (lower right photo). They provide a hint that these planes may soon be secured and tethered below deck until their next mission.

A-6 Intruders can make perfect recoveries, too. The LSOs overseeing the approach of this incoming aircraft must be convinced that its pilot has carrier landings down to a science; their poses reflect a total lack of anxiety over his performance. The LSOs' impression of a pilot's abilities can be crucial to the pilot's career. The LSO is the pilot's final judge and gives the pilot his marks after the recovery. The LSO then records these grades in a confidential log. The pilot of this Intruder would most likely receive a grade of "OK" for a perfect approach and landing. The deceptive mark of "C" would be given in the event of a poor approach.

Shown at the moment when its tailhook is just trapping the arresting cable, this A-6 (upper left photo) is assisted in its recovery by the unique split wing-tip braking system. This rear view of an Intruder's tailhook yanking an arresting cable (upper right photo) illustrates the degree of stress inflicted on these cables when they are hooked. Though constructed of strands of steel, arresting cables have snapped in the past and are capable of slicing a crewman in half. The actual length of the cables is not apparent here. In fact, threaded through a number of slow-down reels in the hull and connecting to hydraulic pistons below deck, there is sixteen times the amount of the visible cable that runs across the deck to trap the aircraft. Once the Intruder is unfettered from the cable, it rolls clear of the landing deck, toward awaiting crew members who have taken refuge near the tail of an EA-6B Prowler (lower photo).

Routine maintenance and major repairs go on both night and day directly below the flight deck in the spacious hangar deck. This nether world of steel ceiling, pipes and storage racks, miscellaneous equipment and yellow "mules" covers an area of about two acres.If necessary, it can store at least two dozen aircraft. As these photos attest, planes in need of repair are arranged in the most space-efficient manner possible. Now and then you come across some equipment that might not be government issue (note the cabin cruisers sitting on props at the left rear [right photo]). "200" Tomcatter sits alone, nestled in a corner of the hangar deck against a wall bearing the colorful insignia of the FORRESTAL. Notice the variety of fuel tanks stored in the racks overhead (lower photo).

Weather permitting, and if they are not complex, repairs and maintenance can be carried in a secluded area of the deck. Here minor on-deck repairs are performed on an E-2C (upper left photo), an F-14A (upper right photo) and an S-3 (lower photo). The green shirts appear to have found something amiss with the light on the left tail of the F-14A and, working in tandem, employ their specialized tools to make an adjustment. The S-3's brown-shirted plane captains are joined by a security officer and a green shirt in an effort to make this Viking airworthy.

Far removed from the Mediterranean Sea near Turkey, this green-helmeted maintenance man does some close-up sanding work on the wing of an aircraft while the FORRESTAL is in the port at Marseille harbor (upper photo). The presence of the mule tractor next to this Tomcat , and the yellow tow bar attached to the aircraft's nosewheel, hint that this F-14 may be on its way to the hangar deck for service that cannot be performed on deck.

There is plenty of open space on the flight deck for maintenance crew to operate, particularly in the area around the island. Here is an example of how the aircraft are situated nose to nose when stored on deck. Notice how the yellow wheel chocks can be used for other than their designed purpose; someone has set up several of them as boundary markers near the darkly-painted SH-2 Seasprite helicopter.

Following its landing, this F-14 of the "Red Rippers" is towed to the stern for a check-up. As it maneuvers past the nose of the E-2C Hawkeye, a couple of crewmen pass some free time admiring the visiting French "Lynx" helicopter that has landed on board.

The setting sun has turned an otherwise mundane scene into something extraordinary. While these deck hands go about their routine, unaware that anything out of the ordinary is occurring, the sun's rays transform the catapult rail running beneath these Tomcats into a golden pathway capable of leading these aircraft to celestial heights known to only a select few. The mysterious aura of this steamy, shadowy world makes it difficult to believe that such humdrum activity as maintenance and repair takes place here.

The colorful insignia of USS FORRESTAL, seen here in the form of an embroidered patch.

The planes that embark on board an aircraft carrier are the ship's main line of offence and defence. During its operational life, a carrier like the FORRESTAL may have several air wings associated with it. The multi-colored patch displayed here is the emblem of the air group that became permanently attached to the FORRESTAL: Carrier Air Wing SIX (CAW-6). CAW-6 is composed of 9 squadrons, totalling about 85 aircraft. These squadrons are: Fighter Squadron THIRTY-ONE (VF-31) and Fighter Squadron ELEVEN (VF-11) flying the F-14 Tomcat; Strike Fighter Squadron ONE THIRTY-TWO (VFA-132) and Strike-Fighter Squadron ONE THIRTY-SEVEN (VFA-137) flying the F/A-18 Hornet; Attack Squadron ONE HUNDRED SEVENTY-SIX (VA-176) flying the A-6 Intruder; Tactical Electronic Warfare Squadron ONE THIRTY-THREE (VAQ-133) flying the EA-6B Prowler; Air Anti-Submarine Squadron TWENTY-EIGHT (VS-28) flying the S-3 Viking; Carrier Airborne Early Warning Squadron ONE HUNDRED TWENTY-TWO (VAW-122) flying the E-2C Hawkeye; and Helicopter Anti-Submarine Squadron FIFTEEN (HS-15) flying the SH-3H Sea King helicopter.

VF-31, nicknamed the "Tomcatters", have F-14s which sport the vertical tail insignia of the cartoon character Felix the Cat. Felix has been seen aboard the FORRESTAL for nearly three decades. The number at the top of the tail is the identification number for the plane relative to its squadron. The numbers "00", "01" and "02" are reserved for the squadron leader or Commander Air Group (CAG). Planes bearing these designations usually retain the colorful paint jobs popular in the Navy during the 1960s.

VF-11, known as the "Red Rippers", decorates the tails of its Tomcats with its unique insignia—the wild boar. Usually the aircraft in CAW-6 have two large letters painted on their tails "AE". The "A" stands for the Atlantic fleet of which the FORRESTAL is a part; the "E" is the code letter for Air Wing 6.

The tails of two A-6 Intruders of VA-176, the "Thunderbolts". Here is an excellent example of two paint schemes: the high-visibility light gray/white with bright squadron insignia and the low-visibility dull gray with subdued insignia. It is an open question whether the low-viz camouflage scheme required on many of today's Navy aircraft replaces the high-viz paint jobs at a risk to the esprit de corps of the squadrons.

VFA-137 has the squadron nickname of the "Kestrels" (also known as the Fleet Falcons, which explains the squadron's avian tail decoration seen here). Notice the air wing designation and the carrier affiliation painted below "Navy".

This badge can only belong to one squadron—VAW-122, the "Steeljaws". It is unknown whether this squadron's E-2Cs will ever have to comply with the sweeping trend to subdue squadron badges and national insignia on military aircraft; their functions do not bring them in view of enemy aircraft so a low-viz paint scheme seems unnecessary.

The "Aces and Eights" card hand adorning the tail of this plane identifies it as an S-3 Viking of VS-28, known as the "Gamblers".

The wild boar insignia of VF-11's "Red Rippers" depicted by these embroidered patches, is one of two insignia embellishing the tails of F-14 Tomcats aboard the FORRESTAL.

The F-14 Tomcat is the two-seat, twin engine, all-weather supersonic aircraft popularized by last decade's successful movie "Top Gun". During the Vietnam War, the performance of the F-8 Crusader and the F-4 Phantom proved unsatisfactory. Following that conflict, Grumman was contracted to design a new fighter the result being the F-14. The first time a Tomcat was tested in combat was on August 19, 1981 when two F-14s engaged two Libyan jets over the Gulf of Sidra. When one of the Libyans fired a missile at the F-14s, they shot down both Libyan aircraft. Since then, Tomcats have participated in a number of patrols related to the taking of hostages and performed well during the Persian Gulf War.

The F-14 is powered by two Pratt & Whitney TF30-P-414A turbofan engines, providing this Tomcat with over 40,000 lbs of thrust. While it appeared for a time that a new F-14D variant would be produced, complete with even more powerful General Electric F110 turbofans and a host of updated electronic gadgetry to improve navigation and intelligence distribution, the defence budget cuts of 1991 scrapped these plans.

All cleaned up and ready to go. This particular F-14 of the "Red Rippers" represents what every aircraft enthusiast and pilot sees in his mind when he envisions a Tomcat. Notice that the high-visibility paint scheme includes atypical red triangles above the fold-out steps. Beneath the number "104" on the nose is the muzzle blast trough for the 20mm Vulcan M61 "Gatling"-style rotary cannon which is part of the F-14's weapon system. Directly below that, underneath the nose, is the Northrop TVSU (television sight unit) which scans a 30-degree field of view to track and identify enemy aircraft.

This patch (left photo), showing Felix the Cat carrying a bomb, complete with a sizzling fuse, to a nearby (we hope) target, is an example of the same insignia that appears on the tail of the planes belonging to VF-31 (see lower photo). This squadron has been painting the emblem of Felix the Cat on its aircraft since the 1930s. The other patch (right photo) is a lesser known variation of insignia for this squadron.

Perched precariously close to the edge of the FORRESTAL's deck, this F-14 (upper left photo) is painted in a subdued tone of light gray, with low-viz national insignia and "Tomcatter" tail badge. It provides an illustration of the Tomcat's unique variable-geometry wings which can be swept back to 75 degrees and overlap its tailplanes for better deck storage (upper left and lower photo). The F-14 has a maximum in-flight sweep of 68 degrees to enable it to achieve supersonic flight (upper right photo).

"Tomcatter" "202" gives maximum power to his engines just prior to launch and prepares for a flight that can reach a speed of Mach 2.34 over twice the speed of sound. Underneath the wings are two 267-gallon external fuel tanks which allow the F-14 to achieve a maximum unrefuelled range of 2400 miles.

These mottled-gray Tomcats from both VF-31 and VF-11 are more than a match for any enemy aircraft with a Sidewinder and a white-nosed AIM-7 Sparrow missile under their wings. The F-14 is designed to carry a destructive array of munitions. These aircraft can carry four AIM-54 Phoenix missiles mounted on pallets, or four AIM-7 Sparrow missiles fitted underneath the fuselage. The underwing pylons can hold different combinations of missiles too.

Almost as if its a showpiece, a nicely painted F-14 of VF-31 sits chained and chocked to the deck of the FORRESTAL in Marseille harbor, proudly displaying its full-color national insignia and bright red "Tomcatters" tail emblem. Note the refuelling probe that extends from the nose just at the front of the canopy.

Gray and graceful as a seagull, this sleek "Tomcatter" soars high above clouds, with a crew that is anxious to carry out their mission (upper photo). The two-man crew of the F-14 the pilot and RIO (radio intercept officer) are highly trained and educated in their particular job; the complexity and sophistication of the machine they control compels them to be. The crew has at their disposal the Hughes AN/AWG-9 pulse-Dopple radar system which is capable of tracking up to 24 targets simultaneously and can detect fighter-sized aircraft at a distance of up to 195 miles. With the aid of the Northrop camera sight located under the Tomcat's nose (which gives the RIO a magnified image of the "bogey" picked up on radar), the crew can attack six of the enemy targets at one time. Considering the potentially fatal "greetings" that these men have the power to unleash, we can be glad we are receiving their wave and visor-covered smiles (right photo).

68

Looking much like a parking lot operated by valets with no organizational skills, the deck of the FORRESTAL appears cluttered with a great gray and off-white jumble of all types of aircraft. There should be no doubt, however, that each of these planes is exactly where it belongs, with its location known to the flight deck control center and all those who will eventually direct their movement.

An embroidered squadron patch of VFA-132, the "Privateers", which features an overhead view of the F/A-18 Hornet flown by them. The current insignia that adorns the tails of their aircraft is a full-sailed schooner with two F-18s shooting straight up past the ship. In the late 1980s, the insignia they bore was the bust of a pirate, complete with eye-patch and tricorn hat.

The F/A-18 Hornet, designed by McDonnell-Douglas, is a dual jet engine, fighter/attack bomber aircraft which is destined to completely replace the A-7 Corsair on board aircraft carriers. Hornets of VFA-132 figured prominently in the retaliatory air strikes against Libya ordered by President Reagan in 1986 when the squadron was attached to the USS CORAL SEA. The F/A-18s of the "Privateers" eventually settled in on the FORRESTAL, as the large white "59" of the super carrier (seen beyond the Hornet in the foreground) attests.

A small collection of Hornets receives attention from various flight deck crewmen prior to launch. Notice that the wings of the F/A-18s also fold to insure maximum storage ability; the wings won't be unfolded to their full span until just before launching. This vantage point provides a clear view of the lift-generating leading edge extension (LEX) section of the wings which can be seen to terminate just below the front of the canopy bubble. Another unique visible trait of the F/A-18s of the "Privateers" is the use of calligraphy to designate the modex and squadron number of the planes.

The pilot of this "Privateers" Hornet appears to be acknowledging a signal from an unseen flight director. Certainly ready for action, the F/A-18 is powered by two General Electric F404 afterburning turbofans which put out 16,000 pounds of thrust each.

The squadron emblem on the tail of this Hornet of VFA-132 is in the low-chroma paint scheme, along with the rest of markings on this plane. The pale white national insignia can be seen underneath the leading edge extension strake below the pilot. Notice that the modex on the nose in the "300" range of numbers; the VF-132 F/A-18s on the FORRESTAL were assigned identification numbers between 300 and 312.

The yellow-tipped nose of this Hornet houses the fighter's AN/APG-65 multi-mode digital tracking radar which is used for ground attack as well as long-range air-to-air intercepts. It is able to track ten targets simultaneously, while displaying eight of them to the pilot. Aside from radar weaponry, the F/A-18 can mount a separate arsenal of offensive weapons. Like the F-14, the Hornet is also armed with the M61 Vulcan 20mm rotary cannon, the black holes of its muzzle being visible at the rear of the radome on top of the plane's nose. The F/A-18 can be armed with several air-to-air missiles which include the AIM-7 Sparrow, the AIM-9 Sidewinder and the AIM-120 AMRAAM; for air-to-ground strikes Hornets can carry AGM-65 Mavericks with a AN/ASQ-173 laser spot tracker/strike camera. More options are the AN/AAS-38 FLIR (infrared intelligence-gathering equipment) and AGM-84 Harpoon anti-ship missiles. Notice the Sidewinder loaded onto the left wing tip station.

There is plenty of room aboard the FORRESTAL for this Hornet to share some deck space with at least a couple of other CAW-6 aircraft, though the Prowler and the Intruder seem to have segregated themselves from the Hornet; perhaps they feel superior because the F/A-18 lacks the refueling probe so prominently displayed by the other two. The Hornet has an in-flight refueling probe, too, but it is retractable and hidden in its nose.

The first attractive patch of VFA-137, the "Kestrels" (left photo), features the profile of a falcon and three tiny red F/A-18s climbing skyward, leaving exhaust trails in their wake. This variation of the squadron patch (right photo) displays the menacing image of a Hornet screaming straight at the viewer.

A couple of plane captains look after their charges while awaiting some mules to tow them to the catapult area. The F/A-18s belonging to the "Kestrels" have been coded with numbers ranging from 400 to 412 and that is how the flight crews and Air Boss will refer to them during their missions. Notice that the pilot ladders extend down from the left LEX; being an integral part of the aircraft, it is stored underneath that section of the wing when not in use. The red line seemingly shooting out from the front of the canopy of the Hornet at the far left is the retractable in-flight fueling probe.

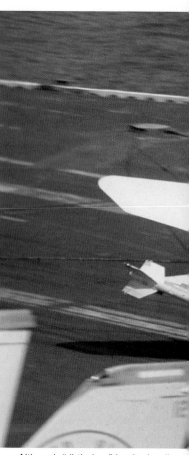

Although "dirtied up" by the landing
land on aircraft carriers because of the d
emblem on the angled tail fin is brightly d

hook, these F/A-18s manage to retain a substantial amount of their trim in-flight appearance. Hornets have been described as being "particularly pleasant" to :rol and stability the pilot is able to exercise over the aircraft. The beautifully, more traditionally painted Hornet "400" belongs to the VFA-137. Notice that the e appellation of "Fleet Falcons" is stenciled onto the external fueling tank under his right wing.

The pilots of these F/A-18s (one from each of the strike-fighter squadrons) take a launch position in their respective cockpits prior being catapulted off of the deck. While Tomcat pilots can hold on to the stick and throttle during a launch, Hornet pilots are required to grab hold of the instrument panel cover. This is a successful means of resisting the physical strain caused by the launch. Because the Hornet has a lighter frame weight compared to the F-14, its launch creates a more intense G-load.

The A-6 Intruder is a low level all-weather carrier attack bomber designed by Grumman. On an attack mission it can carry five 2,000 pound Mk84 general purpose bombs or a maximum of twenty-eight 500 pound bombs, and drop them accurately on a target regardless of inclement weather or darkness. The Intruder began its highly successful career in 1963, and during the Vietnam War delivered many devastating blows to North Vietnam, often at night. Pilots and flight crews of the A-6E have every reason to be proud of the heritage of the birds they handle.

This star-studded patch with the fiery red lightning bolt slashing through it is the insignia for VA-176, aptly nicknamed the "Thunderbolts" (left photo). This squadron flies A-6E Intruders. The second patch (right photo) is designed to convey the message that the A-6E is a bird that has a supernormal ability to find and destroy its prey.

Spreading its red-striped wings for flight, this A-6 wends its way skyward. The Intruders aboard the FORRESTAL are numbered with a "500" series modex; the "00" of the squadron commander is taking off here. It is interesting and unusual that the squadron commander's plane of VA-176 is so drab in its paint scheme.

The KA-6D is a special fuel tanker version of the A-6, developed specifically to help extend the range of fighter and attack aircraft, which has a 16,000 pound refueling capacity. Note the propeller-tipped Sargent-Fletcher D704 "buddy" in-flight refueling pack visible at tire level below the belly of Intruder "523" (upper photo). The KA-6D can be distinguished from the A-6E by the housing for the hose and reel refueling system, located on the right side of the fuselage below the word "Navy" (lower right photo). The housing is a conversion of the outmoded perforated air brake (the small black holes) seen on each side of the aircraft.

The A-6E had its maiden flight on November 10, 1970. Its distinctive profile large nose and canopy area slimming drastically to the narrow region at the tail is well depicted here (upper photo). The A6-E's trademark, its large refueling probe, sits directly in front of the windscreen, atop and to the rear of the bulbous nose radome (lower photo). Inside the radome are crammed the Norden APQ-148 multi-mode radar and other avionics that enable the Intruder to map the terrain below the aircraft and identify and track targets. With so many technological devices gathered in one place, it is easy to understand how the aircraft came to look so nose heavy.

Due to the likelihood that the A-6E's position will be sought by the enemy aircraft during its wartime operations, the regulation paint scheme of light gray over white has fallen victim to the exigencies of camouflage. The drab appearance of these Intruders is offset only by the red paint on the pilot's ladder and wing supports.The small turret-like fairing beneath the radome is the TRAM (Target Recognition Attack, Multisensor) which houses the equipment known as FLIR (Forward Looking Infrared), the laser rangefinder and tracker system.

The Intruder tanker has four 400 gallon fuel tanks attached to the underside of its wings.

These A-6s have managed to avoid the change to muted gray tones, at least temporarily. These Intruders do exhibit some evidence of outward wear and tear, however, and this brown shirt is going the extra mile to make sure that they shine in honor of the FORRESTAL's final deployment. Awaiting a tow to the catapults, the aircraft are laden with underwing fuel tanks. The two Pratt & Whitney J52-8B turbojets that power the A-6s will put that fuel to good use, providing the aircraft with over 9000 pounds of thrust and sustaining their flight for a range of some 1011 miles.

In a face to face encounter with this KA-6D, it seems to bear a striking resemblance to some kind of giant insect, complete with antenna (refueling probe) and bug-like eyes (canopy windscreen). Of course, it might have conveyed a less entomological appearance if the plane's windscreen provided a clearer view of the pilot and bombardier/navigator from this angle.

With its wheels chocked, intake covers on and wings folded, this KA-6D takes in some sun during a break in operations. With a wingspan of 53 feet, it is more convenient and efficient to fold the wings to the compact size of 25 feet 4 inches when the plane is stowed on deck. This tanker Intruder exhibits a first-class appearance and has somehow managed to avoid the application of a coat of flat gray paint. One alteration to its outward paint scheme is unavoidable—the removal of the USS FORRESTAL designation on the side of its fuselage.

VAQ-133, which employs the moniker of the "Wizzards", is a tactical electronic warfare squadron, as these patches so vibrantly indicate. Their main goal is to disrupt the effectiveness of the enemy's radar and communication systems. The aircraft flown by this unit is the EA-6B Prowler (lower photo), a 4-seat variation of the A-6 which possesses enormous ECM (electronic countermeasure) capabilities. The first Prowler flew in 1968 and the most recent opportunity the EA-6B had to flex its electronic muscle on a grand scale was during the Persian Gulf War. The Prowler bears the symbol for radiation on its nose so that the LSOs can differentiate it from the A-6 during a landing.

Like its cousin the A-6, this dusty gray EA-6B, seen here in action off the coast of southern Turkey, has a most distinctive profile. However, the protruding refueling probe on top of the nose seems miniscule in size compared to the bulging tip of the Prowler's vertical tail. This bulge houses ECM surveillance receivers used for long-range detection of radar. Other antennae are hidden by a multitude of bumps and welts under the wings and on the tail. The Prowler's principal weapon is the ANL ALQ-99 high-power jamming system contained in a pod that hangs from pylons under the wings, five of which can be attached to these aircraft. These pods are recognizable by the small nose propeller which spins in flight to produce power to the jamming system.

The enlarged cockpit of Prowler "623" is typical of all EA-6Bs and is home to a 4-man crew of electronic warfare officers (EWOs). The senior EWO operates half of the system's frequency coverage while the man behind him handles the other half. Behind the pilot, a third EWO employs the jamming system to disrupt the source of the radio and radar signals. Somewhat symbolically, the camera has captured the reflection of sunlight off the Prowler's canopy. The temporary visual blindness caused by the reflection could be considered figurative of the electronic "blindness" these men produce during their mission.

Once it is launched, this EA-6B Prowler, powered by Pratt & Whitney J52-P-408 turbojet engines, will be able to reach a level flying speed in excess of 500 knots. Because of the Prowler's swollen tail fin, displayed to advantage here (left photo), naval aircraft enthusiasts have little trouble distinguishing it from the other military aircraft used by the government, particularly the A-6. Because of the costly collection of ECM equipment it contains, the EA-6B is well known to government purchasers of aircraft, too. This Prowler ascending upward from the flight deck is not the only thing that is sky high; the price tag for the plane is over $100,000,000.

The patches of VS-28 illustrate the squadron's ties with the past, even though they undertake some of the most technologically modern warfare of any flying group on the FORRESTAL. Appropriately, the "Gamblers" of VS-28 have adopted the historic "dead-man's hand" of aces and eights as their squadron emblem; on the one patch they have added a sleepy young lady who was the subject of numerous popular "Varga girl" nose art portraits during World War II. Aboard the FORRESTAL, VS-28 flies S-3A Viking anti-submarine warfare (ASW) aircraft designed by Lockheed.

Its flight having been powered by two 9280 lb thrust General Electric TF34 turbofan engines (that are positioned notably close to the fuselage), this S-3 is seconds away from trapping back on board. The Viking has an internal fuel capacity of 1900 gallons which provides the aircraft with a typical range of 2000 nautical miles and an unrefuelled flying time of about 4.5 hours.

The design of the S-3's high-aspect ratio wings is unique in that they fold at about mid-point on each side, the wing tips nearly crossing over themselves, thereby reducing the plane's nearly 70 ft. wingspan to just under 30 ft. while on deck or stored below. At the very tip of each wing can be seen a wing port that houses ECM antennae.

While attached to the FORRESTAL, the VS-28 is recognized by the '700" series modex on their Vikings. Seen here with its nosewheel launch bar hooked up for action, Viking "706" presents a gray and white paint scheme that is no longer representative of all the planes in the squadron.

This S-3 is hardly recognizable with its wings and its tail fin folded. Seeing the plane in this condition, the viewer is not apt to believe that the Viking could pack much of a punch at all. Nevertheless, inside its dissected exterior is the internal weapons bay which can carry up to 2000 pounds of depth charges, bombs and torpedoes. Dozens of sonobuoys can be loaded into the plane's belly to later be dropped over an area at sea to detect the presence of a submarine. Wing racks can also be loaded with Harpoon anti-ship missiles. As if that weren't enough, the Viking carries a retractable magnetic anamoly detector (MAD) in its tail for searching out submerged enemy submarines, and is equipped with the FLIR and electronic surveillance devices.

Behind this black window operates perhaps the most highly trained group of men that could occupy the cockpit of a modern Navy aircraft—the S-3 Viking's crew of four. Prior to active duty on an S-3, they go through a ten-month training course to learn the intricacies of the aircraft's equipment and how to work as a coordinated unit. The crew is composed of a pilot, co-pilot, tactical coordinator and a sensor operator. The tactical coordinator (TACCO) sits in the right rear seat where he deploys buoys, directs the movement of the aircraft and manages the attack on enemy submarines. The co-pilot (COTAC) functions as a back-up pilot and a TACCO. The sensor operator (SENSO) is the only crew member of enlisted rank. His main responsibility is to analyze acoustic signatures that are processed through the ASW equipment, identify the enemy sub, determine its depth and track its speed.

The menacing design of the patches worn by personnel of VAW-122 reflects quite accurately their nickname of "Steeljaws". The squadron flies the Grumman E-2C Hawkeye, a carrier airborne all-weather aircraft which provides the carrier battlegroup with early-warning surveillance of approaching enemy ships and aircraft, and to direct the carrier's aircraft to the interception point.

Just as the shark on the squadron's emblem (seen to the left of the pilot's window) is most often recognized by his dorsal fin, the most conspicuous feature of the E-2C is the huge rotating radar dome which sits on the back of the Hawkeye. Another outstanding visual aspect of the E-2C is the design of its wings. This aircraft has the impressive wing span of over 80 ft. and can only be towed and stored aboard the FORRESTAL because the wings are hinged is such a way as to allow each wing to bend backwards and rest parallel with the fuselage. Notice that the two-tone paint schemes on these Steeljaws bear full-color national insignia and even a red stripe around the fuselage.

The E-2C, nicknamed the "Hummer", is powered by two 4600 HP Allison turboprop engines which drive two four-blade Hamilton Standard fully-feathering, reversible, constant speed propellers, which are constructed of a combination of steel and foam/glassfiber. Note the large intake positioned behind the large canopy which provides air for the aircraft's cooling system. Combined as one system, they succeed in generating the lift necessary to keep the largest carrier aircraft in the world airborne.

Enclosed in the Randtron AN/APA-171 rotodome, radar can track more than 600 targets simultaneously and control more than 20 intercepts. New production E-2Cs are equipped with the AN/APS-145 radar which is superior to the early 125 version, or even the 139 which enabled the plane's crew to track targets over land and sea at a distance of 300 miles at 30,000 feet.

With its tailhook lowered for recovery, this E-2C trails a train of black smoke from its Allison motors as it approaches the deck of the FORRESTAL. The E-2C is crewed by a group of five:- pilot and co-pilot, of course, and three "moles": combat information center officer, air control officer, and radar operator who manage to cram themselves into the dark confines of the cockpit. After recovery from a typical four-hour mission, the moles have a difficult time adjusting the light of day. When necessary, the Hawkeye can operate on automatic pilot. In July of 1991, a fire in the starboard engine of an E-2C of VAW-122 flying off the FORRESTAL compelled the crew to bail out and as the aircraft flew on automatic toward the populated coast, an F/A-18 shot it down.

Standing still and giving this E-2C plenty of room to maneuver, it is likely that these crew members are keeping a healthy distance from the whirling props of this Hawkeye. Or perhaps they fear the ferocious visage of the shark badge displayed on the tail fin. Notice that the tail fins of the E-2C are unlike those of any other Navy aircraft. At the time it was designed, in order to prevent the tail fins from interfering with the radar, the large vertical tail was rejected in favor of a group of four small tails .

The official (left photo) and unofficial (right photo) badges of HS-15, the "Red Lions". Notice that the unofficial patch is adorned with the "Varga girl" seen on the patch of the VS-28 "Gamblers". HS-15 flies the Sikorsky SH-3H Sea King which is a gas-turbine powered helicopter used for anti-submarine warfare and rescue and assistance missions. The Sea King is also commonly used to transfer cargo and personnel between ships at sea. There are five of these helicopters in HS-15 while attached to CAW-6.

These images show the Sea King's large rotor blades which extend to a 62 ft. circle. The maintenance men swarming over the rotor itself provide a scale by which we can measure the height of the helicopter. Though smaller in diameter, the five tail rotor blades are no less impressive (right photo). The low-visibility dark gray paint scheme on "Red Lions" "612" is noteworthy.

As it hovers over the FORRESTAL's deck, this SH-3H offers an excellent view of its underside. Though not specifically designed to be set down in the ocean, the Sea King does have a watertight bottom. This feature, plus buoyancy bags carried in the stabilizing floats (seen here just above the landing gear), could go a long way toward helping the crew survive a forced landing at sea.

Sea King helicopters are airborne during all flight operations from the FORRESTAL. This is a measure taken to insure the safety and recovery of any airplane crew that might be forced to eject into the ocean. The SH-3H is capable of remaining airborne for more than five hours.

As the Sea King descends for a landing, this chopper crewman keeps a sharp watch on the aircraft parked on the FORRESTAL's deck from his station at the door in the body of the helicopter (left photo). Wearing helmets emblazoned with a rampant red lion, and with their bright squadron patches sewn to their flight suits, crew members of HS-15 walk with a determined stride after returning from their mission (right photo). Whether in their capacity as anti-submarine warriors, transport personnel or rescue patrolmen, the crew members of the SH-3H are as invaluable to the success of flight operations as any fixed-wing crewman flying from the decks of Navy carriers.

The subtle differences in its design, and the presence of yellow and red stripes on its body, betray this helicopter as belonging to a different squadron. Indeed, this SH-2 Seasprite hails from HSL-32 of the cruiser USS YORKTOWN (as so indicated on the left stabilizing float) which escorted the FORRESTAL for a few days. Apart from the sonar, sonobuoys, homing torpedoes and depth bombs that Sea Kings can employ in their anti-submarine activity, they are also equipped with a magnetic anamoly detection (MAD) device (the yellow and red "funnel" seen in upper right and lower photos extending from the rear of the starboard stabilizing float). The MAD picks up the distortion to the Earth's magnetic field caused by the submarine's presence, allowing the SH-2 to get a fix on the undersea vessel.

Another visitor, this time a Lynx helicopter of the Marine Nationale (French navy) attached to the French destroyer "Jean de Vienne", finds a home away from home on the deck of the FORRESTAL. Smaller in size than the Sea King, the Lynx only requires four rotor blades to take it aloft.

The C-2 Greyhound is a sort of cousin to the E-2C Hawkeye, closely resembling it in appearance. The C-2 is not part of CAW-6 but provides invaluable transportation services between ship and shore during the time of an aircraft carrier's deployment . This is the reason the C-2 is often referred to as a COD (Carrier On-board Delivery).

Seemingly ready to devour one of the personnel of an air base in Turkey, the Greyhound opens its ample fuselage to receive its load. The C-2 can carry 39 passengers or 10,000 pounds of cargo. It is a popular aircraft with the carrier's crew members because one of its duties is to bring aboard bags of long-awaited mail from home.

The T56-A-425 engines which power the C-2 Greyhound spin massive four-blade propellers which, along with the wings that fold parallel, the small vertical fins and the light gray/white color scheme, account for the similarities between the C-2 and the E-2C. Note the large "COD" which the Greyhound exhibits on the right side of the starboard engine.

Several differences in physical features differentiate the C-2 from the E-2C, most notably the absence of the Hawkeye's massive rotodome. Also missing is the air intake above the canopy. The stubbier nose of the Greyhound, when combined with its increased girth, gives the C-2 a sluggish demeanor that belies the fact that it is an efficient and reliable delivery aircraft.

The A-7 Corsair made its last cruise aboard the FORRESTAL in the winter of 1989-1990. Two fighter squadrons were on board : VA-37, the "Bulls", and VA-105, the "Gunslingers". Corsairs bearing the squadron emblem for the"Bulls", a rampaging bull (upper photo), and the tail insignia for the "Gunslingers", the chess piece trademark of the television gunfighter Paladin (right photo), have since become a part of the FORRESTAL's history.

With a "thumbs-up", this pilot shows he is ready to take what could be his last flight in the cockpit of a Corsair, F/A-18s being the Navy's preferred light attack aircraft now. This single-engine jet aircraft, which was primarily used for close air support and attack, has its cockpit in the forward nose of the plane. This accords the pilot excellent forward in-flight and landing visiblity. The A-7 was one of the first aircraft equipped with the head up display (HUD) which can be seen here on top of the instrument panel. Note the retractable refuelling probe, appearing here as a pipe running under the pilot's name.

The Corsair is famous for its snub nose and the nose intake that runs beneath it, both of which combine to give the A-7 its unattractive, almost comical look. Despite its appearance, the Corsair is a reliable aircraft and popular with pilots. The engine that propels it is a single Allison TF41 turbofan which produces 15,000 pounds of thrust and can take the plane to a top sea level speed of nearly 700 mph. Notice that the cavernous nose intake of the A-7 in right photo is somewhat elaborately covered by a screen. This is a necessary safety precaution when the pilot is revving the engine as the intake poses the very real threat of inhaling any careless deck hand who might wander too close.

Arguably, there is little about this drably painted "Bull" of VA-37 , sitting here the the FORRESTAL's deck in Marseille harbor, its hinged wings folded just like any other carrier aircraft, that could engender the respect that this aircraft merits. Even its size works against it; the A-7 has the distinction of being the smallest plane on a carrier. Its wingspan is just under 40 ft. and it is only a little over 16 ft. tall. Although not impressive to behold, once its ordnance is loaded the A-7 becomes a formidable war machine. Externally, it can carry over 15,000 pounds of bombs, missiles and rockets. It is also equipped with an internal 20mm Vulcan cannon which shoots from the Corsair's lower port side.

This ghostly A-7 being towed to its resting place symbolizes the end of a proud role in naval aviation, both for the Corsair and for the USS FORRESTAL. Just like many other famous aircraft throughout history, the A-7 Corsair has succumbed to innovations in aviation design and technology. As of the printing of this book, the FORRESTAL, the first "super carrier", has reached the end of its active military life, too. Both will be fondly remembered.

1:144 Series

4003 F/A-18A w/CARRIER DECK (BLAST-OFF)

4006 A-6E & F/A-18A (LIBYAN RAIDERS)

4007 F-14A vs F-16N (TOP GUN)

4019 F-14A w/GROUND SUPPORT EQUIPMENT (FIGHTERTOWN USA/NAS MIRAMAR)

4020 F-14A w/DECK VEHICLES (LAUNCH!)

4552 F-14A WOLF PACK CAG 'VF-1'

4559 F-14D TOMCAT 'VF-31 TOMCATERS'

4569 A-6E INTRUDER 'VMA-533 HAWK'

"STEPS AHEAD..... ALWAYS"

DML
PLASTIC MODEL KITS

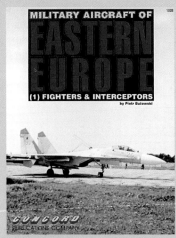

1028 Military Aircraft of Eastern Europe: (1) Fighters & Intercepters
by Piotr Butowski

1029 U.S. Navy's Strike Warfare Center
by Barry D. Smith

1032 Maple Flag
by Mike Reyno

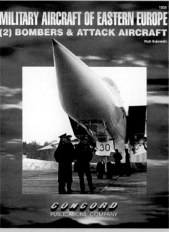

1035 Military Aircraft of Eastern Europe: (2) Bombers & Attack Aircraft
by Piotr Butowski

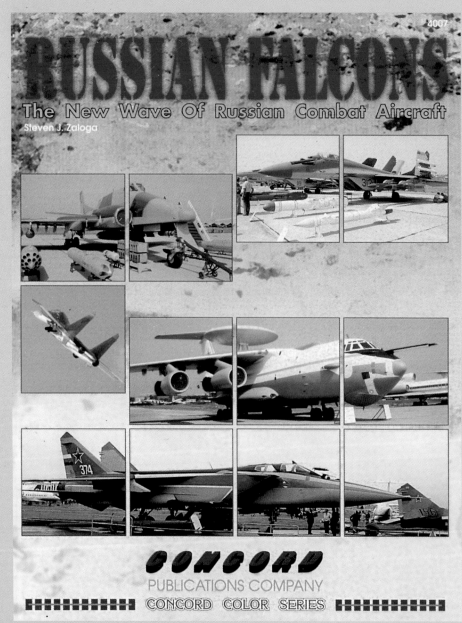

4007 Russian Falcons: The New Wave of Russian Combat Aircraft
by Steven J. Zaloga

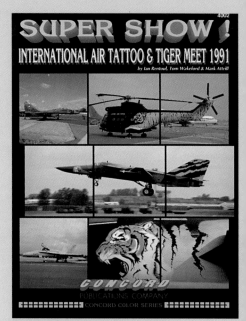

4002 Super Show!
International Air Tattoo & Tiger Meet 1991
by Ian Rentoul, Tom Wakeford & Mark Attrill

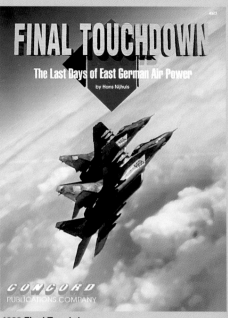

4003 Final Touchdown:
The Last Days of East German Air Power
by Hans Nijhuis

CONCORD
PUBLICATIONS COMPANY